AF317053

I'm Sick

I'm Sick

(Is it all I'll ever be?)

Thomas Hennessy

CONTENTS

CONTENTS

CONTENTS

CONTENTS

CONTENTS

1

Intro

My name is Tom Hennessy. Welcome to a collection of my poetry. I have been writing poetry for some time now, as a coping skill for my anxiety and addiction. I'm so excited to share with you some of my perspectives on life, as well as some encouragement. Life has been hard, I have no doubt that you can relate. Despite any challenges or struggles, I'm still here, and so are you. As a society, we have come a long way in terms of mental health support. Stigma has drastically decreased, and there is a much bigger voice for people going through similar issues. For that, I am so grateful. No one should ever have to feel like they are struggling alone, and no one should feel as though they aren't deserving of their existence. I want this book to spread some awareness, as sometimes I feel that people forget an important part of recovery. Recovery is not linear, and everyone makes mistakes. The most important part of growing as a person is recognizing that the progress is not over just because you relapsed, or made mistakes. Keep fighting. I love you.

No light at the end of the tunnel

I'm starting to notice a pattern. Things are getting worse. I seem to struggle more and more. life is too complex.

Put up with me
While I put on a show
Nothing more real than an act
Promise you won't go
But it's a fact
No one stays with me

—

Hearts don't just break, they shatter
Broken bones don't hurt like this
Trying to numb this sad clatter
But love isn't for me
Not one more kiss

Distance of Disassociation

When I look in a mirror, I see eyes, a face, me?
Who am I, if not a lie?
Me?
What does that mean?
I'm living in a movie scene, replaying the credits.
As names go by, people cry.
A eulogy?
Why?
Remember someone's lies, or tries.
As far as I can see, I see me.
Me?
What does that mean?
An arbitrary label, to differentiate experiences.
But what have I experienced?
Love? Hate? Indifference?
Afraid of existence or what existence entails.
My body taken out of itself.
Taking everything out, but to make thoughts real.
Simply what is a thought if not proof.
Proof of reality.
I lost my battle with distance and velocity changes as I force myself to come back.
Back to me?
Who is me?
I am not.

In fact no one can be.

Posthumous humors

A dying leaf shrivels and crumples, lost in the pile of thousands more.

Ironic

For that leaf was the most beautiful

And now it is the most ordinary

Post death is when we see the truth, when all our falsities and fallacies come to light

Yet we still celebrate those lives no matter how cold a body is in its grave.

The humor in death is quite exquisite,

But the posthumous humors no longer share the same irony as the leaf

For I was unholy and ugly before death and uglier I get with the shriveled eyes and twisted face.

Lost in the little things I forgot to see the end I was searching for,

And I was not ready anymore but it came anyway

Don't jump

It came to me in a dream like the word of god
Frayed and hot like a burning rope
Calling to my eyes
A vision so cold It stings my sight
Falling from a world ringed with lackluster hope
Only to find that the bubble you once called safe
Is a place of desolation
You fail to let go
Instead
Letting go of the burning rope
Listening to the word of god as he tells you:
Fall forward

Souls

Falling in and out of love
Our souls combine
But I stole part of your soul
And I won't give it back
Taking that with me everywhere
I can't be me without part of you

2

Life is really good
until it's not

I can't say that I'm not happy, yet I still feel like something is missing. Will I get better? Can I?

Hoping to have no regrets

Forget regret
Tales of lament
Insatiable appetites ruin lives
Never content
But regret hurts more than lies

—

Finding hope feels too good
I wish I deserved to believe
But hope twists God's arm
Nothing can cure the world of the devil's mockery
But I'll be laughing along

Can't taste the sweet honey

Was I cursed?
When they left me behind i started to forget
But I missed out
And I fall closer to the edge
Why doesn't the honey make my tea sweet
Bitter doesn't get better
But getting better doesn't change
Just out of reach forever

Balance is everything

Light can not exist without casting a shadow
Empty and desolate is the world barren of light
The same for one void of dark
No ups without downs
For balance is truth
Good creates evil
And evil sustains good

Mania

I think that I'm God
But God doesn't enjoy my fantasy
For I'm troubled
Stuck in my own tragedy
I try not to answer the sickening call
I leave the messages read, until one day
I read them all
And violence tempts

Buried

Awoken by the soft chirp of plenty birds
Eyes struggle open to see nothing
Those aren't birds they are bugs
And you are deep
The bugs snickered as they continued their work
Won't ever see the light again
Found self in the last breaths of air
The dirt is so heavy
Yet there's relief in your disbelief
Alive barely enough to feel yourself dying
And oh dear is it painful
So painful

3

Drowning in my own self loathing

I hate myself sometimes. At this point, it feels like most of the time. I tell myself I can't change. Maybe I can but I need help.

Trash

Walking to the dumpster to discard the memories i was left with

Burning pictures because I let my bridges go up in flames
So full of myself
Memories in the trash
Im in the land of the broken toys where no child plays
Melancholy rain drowns out my hollow chest thumping
You left me here and I left you there but I couldn't find nowhere
I guess the train stopped at its last station
Still selfish
These tears aren't for you
The dumpster is full
I can't get rid of the memories you left me with

Stop digging

Content with resigning to failure
Not going to fuck up again
Yet here we are in the same damn hole I dug myself
Put down the shovel before you bury yourself too deep
Burying myself alive out of spite
Endlessly shoveling through a mountain
The other side never closer
Because every single time it falls on me again
Maybe this mountain crushing me wasn't here before I started digging.

Losing a battle with myself

I lived for everyone else, but I can't live for myself
Yet I can't spend all day waiting to succumb to time
Sweet numbness left behind
In the wake of my evil
I listen to these thoughts, and i know they are mine
I don't like it here, I don't like it anywhere
Nothing but the tears I cry
Live and let live, all I want is to be allowed to die

Forgiven

Tears in the heart of a poor young boy
Left in the rain
His pain treated like a toy
Christmas tends to make him cry
Last December he said he was happy
And for a brief moment, he was
Then he fades to black
Now he is laid to rest

Addiction

Flowing slowly
Falling quickly
The trickle won't stop
Neither does the fight
Fighting to die
Yet dying to get high
then it drips
And I choke
I've said "this is the last time"
Too many times
But I have faith
This is the last time

4

Can't give up yet

I spend too much time fighting myself. It never was a war I could win. War has no winners anyway, but I can't let myself become a casualty.

Furthering my addiction

Addicted to the thrill
Telling God go fuck himself
But he can't quit the pill
Some like the bottle
It's a shame
Some can't quit
But don't show pity for the man with percocet in his mouth
He tastes the xanax as he fades away
He didn't expect it to go so south
But don't show pity for the man with percocet in his mouth

Sisyphus daydreams

Climbing hill after hill
Just to find a mountain taller each time
I'm running out of strength
Muscles tearing again and again
In not getting stronger
Forced to climb up
Wanting so bad to let go
I think I'm Sisyphus
For my boulder is heavy
And I lift it and lift it
But it always falls back down
For my boulder is my own creation

No love

Here are the rules
For she will be your demise
Don't leave your heart in her lying eyes
Don't give trust when all it does is break
Don't love hard for your own sake
Follow these rules
Find your peace
When comes around
The feelings cease

Nowhere

I think I found nowhere
An empty abyss
No child more distant
Searching an endless end
Nowhere to go so we go nowhere
I think I found it
A word with no true meaning
A place that does no dreaming
I think I found nowhere
Let out a scream.
A loud one.
A scream into the growing abyss
But no one can hear it.
Not loud enough.
Or are you just that far lost?

Life sucks

Life's been better
It's also been worse
But no one can tell me
Why it still hurts
Cycling through
Old memories
Just to realize
It's only a tease
For life won't go back
To where I was then
But life just gets worse
And worse again

5

I can't seem to learn
my lesson

There is no right way to live life. There certainly are wrong ways though. I find that mistakes are inevitable, yet I still don't learn.

Breathless

I can't breathe when I see your face
I can't sleep when I hear your voice
Nothing hurts more than losing my place
I ripped your heart out and threw it away
Filling some void in my chest
But all I did was empty it more
Now I count the days
It has been so long since I've done this
But life seems like it would be better if it were shorter
Counting down again
To the day I'll be breathless
Avoiding the places I used to find joy
Because happiness is something I don't deserve
And I try and try again
But I never seem to die

Addiction hurts

I found god in a hospital
But the pills have the devils tongue
Fraying at the seams
Lost inside the poison of my own creation
Dying for a quick death
Empty lungs can't catch breath
Yet the light at the end is so bright
I can't give up the fight
Not yet

Drown you out

Gurgling water in a winding wood
Children don't play this deep
A serene and pleasurable scene
Twisting river deep and gold with the last lights of the sun
No one should play here
On thin ice
But this boy wasn't playing
Alone with his thoughts
Hovering overhead
An angel wearing black
Not a guardian
He wasn't trying to drown
Only drown you out
No one searched
Angry boys shouldn't run away
He won't see another day
The sun is down now
The ice shined in the dim light of the moon
The boy underneath did not

The eyes of god

Death is what life culminates to
Doesn't that motivate you
A lack of complexity in your small view
A sickening climax shattering time
Something we are told in a nursery rhyme
Taught and learned to do no crime
A child walks on a sea of green
The dirt below teeming with life
The eyes that watch remain unseen
The boy feels the blade of a knife
A simple wasp as the boy had thought
Reminder of morals that he bought
Had the flying demon left
The boy would be grateful yet
But now he can never forget
The life he took with his hand shown
No bugs would carefully stand alone
Call it karma or retribution known
Pray that no one kills you for the crime of being small
But detestable gods will show that they see all
For when that boy got stung
And with his hand a smack had rung
That killed the bug which stung him
Fateful child so small and pure
Swollen through and itchy eyes he fears

Soon buzzing is all he hears
A cloud so dark like a godly plague
Following the child as his skin starts to ache
For when that boy killed the wasp
The eyes of god see all

Pain

Glistening knives cut skin
Sharp stones thrown
Sticks stab and tear
But nothing hurts like the pain you make me feel
No one can hurt me like you do
Not even close

6

Hurting myself out of spite

The damage has been done, but I keep piling on the pain. So much is out of my control, so why should I bother? The answer to that question will always evade me.

Hell is personal

I walked down a full city street
No one looked at me
Facing down my regret
This is hell
Estranged from my soul
Trapped just out of reach
Blinking eyes heavy with anguish
Tears tear at the man forgotten
Forgetting himself as well
I sent a final message
A note
A tribute to a life long lived
A battle hard won
But war has no winners
And letters burn when mailed from hell

Trapped

When you close your eyes, where do you go?
Trapped in my mind
I can't let go
Waiting patiently
Erase yourself carefully
Yet stuck where you are
You reap what you sow
Digging two graves
One for me and you
Only begotten
Just to be forgotten
Finally lost (or free)

Angels hold a bloody knife

As long as you can hold on
As the damn day drags on
Iron in the air
As the angel walks by with that bloody knife
Red as a wilted rose
Thicker than water
The angel wasn't meant to show up yet
Dripping with salty sweat
Bittersweet taste in a small boys mouth
Crying as the bright eyed angel drifted from the sky
Would you cry when the angel comes for you with that
bloody knife
Too soon again
As the angel breathes:
Goodbye

Drowning again

Felt I deserved the ocean
So I drowned myself in it
Felt I deserved the sun
So I set myself on fire
Felt I deserved the moon
So I stopped breathing
Felt I deserved it all
So I gave up on everything

Gasoline

Temptation breeds ill-will
Though I fuel the fire
Burning in a damned cycle
Set myself aflame to prove a point
Sweet evil flows and drips
You smell like gasoline
From my nose the feeling rips
The scent was so strong
I'll never forget
That gasoline smell
When I tried to go up in flames

7

Was I always a quitter?

I gave up again. I keep on trying, but for what? I keep being told that it gets better. That's so cliché, but true it seems.

Dementia

Reminiscent of dimming childhood memories
Don't forget to remember
Grasping at a fleeting thought
Just a burning memory
Recall impure
No longer relevant

—

Little tittering animal
Chattering, clacking
Ticking, and clicking
The little thing snickers
As its tooth falls out
And another
And another
And a boy calls out
He's smiling and grinning
He laughs as his teeth fall out

Soar

Icarus never considered what comes next
Achilles had it right
After death
Comes an eternal sky where Icarus can no longer soar
Falling from the sun again
What's more painful than forgetting how to fly
The Gods only knows what went through his head
As he crashed down to the sea

The reaper is myself

Thrilling nights
Harmless fun
Until you see
It's finally begun
The end we once craved
Is starting its course
Making its way to the place you love most
Death doesn't take you
It takes all your friends
And leaves you alone until
He comes again

Sleepless

Savage beasts sing trashy tunes in my head
Can't sleep with this racket
Heart sinks like lead
You weren't sleeping
Because you'll sleep when you're dead

You just get older

Life gets better
They speak so theoretically
It didn't change
I just got older
And their words meant less and less

8

The light at the end of the tunnel might be fire

High hopes dashed upon the rocks. Tossed out with the rest of my good memories. Will I make it to see the future I planned?

Bad dreams

Sleep comes less and less
Dreaming doesn't help my stress
Living a nightmare that doesn't end
Life has been one endless trend
And when I wake up I realize
Life isn't better than my dreams
Yet the nightmare continues
And I sleep less and less

No more cheap thrills

I think I've lost myself without a trace
Can't even say anything to save face
No matter how good the future may be
You can't change the past
And I can't avoid what I have done
Fast thrills and cheap fun
But now I yearn to see the sun
I can't have what I had once
Lost forever, no more

Still falling for you

Jumped so long ago
Never stopped falling
Dropped ego
Found hatred of heights
Is this hell?
Still falling
Don't want to try
I'm not surprised
I lost again
I never win
I don't want to be here
If you won't be here next to me

Sunsets make me upset

I'm jealous of the sun
For he gets more sleep than me
Tired of drinking in the warm rays until they leave me cold
and bitter
Sad that the end of the day came too quick
At night I lie awake waiting for that sleepy sun to rise
So my sleepless night can end and I can join the world again
There's beauty to find in upset sunsets

I wish

The shimmering, flickering, burning sight of eternity
Pulling softly at your hand
Gently breathing your air
You never meant to hurt me
So I forgive even if I can't forget
Love is just some chemicals telling me you seem cool
It's all fake though I'm not a fool
meet me at the bottom when my heart drops
Don't forget about me when I stop

Separating from my mind

More distant than usual
But I don't mean to be
I never meant for this
I'm being delusional
But I don't mean to be
Lost in the agony of artificial bliss
While I see myself from your view
It's nothing new
But I keep myself separate

Scarred

My chest aches from the scars you gave me
But they heal, Right?
Tears in my heart
I won't feel anymore
But I'll always miss you
Drinking and smoking
Throwing out my tolerance
The flowers are no longer filled with pollen
I think the world is broken
My phone ringing
I'm not going to answer
I broke my brain trying to fix it

March

Not quite spring weather
Too cold to be happy
Marching towards eternity
Too warm to give a shit
Why this in between
God only knows

9

It's ok, I'm ok

I made leaps and bounds in progress. Nothing feels as good as success. I'm still here, by miracle or fate.

True hope

Happy to try and willing to fail
But falling doesn't mean the end
For you can get up and try again
You see your struggles as absolute
But don't forget that isn't true
For you can get up and up again
Seeing a brightness
Feeling warmth
Nothing like this
The sun didn't used to shine
No longer detestable
Success is inevitable
Felt hope once again
I missed this feeling